ABC
off to
sea!

Virginie Morgand

 Thames & Hudson

A is for anchor –
let's raise it! Heave-ho!

B is for buoy
that marks where to go.

C

is for
cruise ship that's
sailing away.

D is for dolphins
that frolic and play.

E

is for everyone
– what a fine crew!

F is for flag – it's bright red and brand new.

G

is for

gulls that we pass
on our trip.

H is for helm,
used for steering our ship.

I is for Ivor,
who'll perch on
your hand.

J is for
Jack, who keeps
look-out for land.

K is for keel
that keeps our boat steady.

L
is for 'Look out!'
A shark! Are you ready?

M is for mermaids, long-haired and bright-eyed.

is for nook,
where lost
treasures
might hide.

P is for pirates
– they're friendly,
we hope!

Q

is for quick!
See the sail boats
race by!

R

is for rope,
rather hard
to untie.

S is for swabbing
– that's cleaning the deck.

T is for
trousers – poor
Tom's are a wreck!

U

is for Ulysses,
who likes to catch mice.

V is for view
through the porthole – how nice!

W is the way
that we've carefully planned.

X marks the spot, now let's head home for land...

Y is for yawn as the lighthouse shines bright.

Zzz is for bedtime
– you'll sleep well tonight!

A is for adventure
that's waiting for you,
the next time you want
to sail into the blue...